trotman

REAL LIFE ISSUES:

KT-429-386

EATING

DISORDERS

REAL LIFE ISSUES

Real Life Issues are self-help guides offering information and advice on a range of key issues that matter to teenagers. Each book defines the issue, probes the reader's experience of it and offers ways of understanding and coping with it. Written in a lively and accessible style, Real Life Issues aim to demystify the areas that teenagers find hard to talk about, providing honest facts, practical advice, inspirational quotes, positive reassurance and guidance towards specialist help.

Other titles in the series include:

trotman

REAL LIFE ISSUES:
EATING
DISORDERS

Heather Warner

Real Life Issues: Eating Disorders
This first edition published in 2004 by Trotman and Company Ltd
2 The Green, Richmond, Surrey TW9 1PL

© Trotman and Company Limited 2004

Editorial and Publishing Team
Author Heather Warner
Editorial Mina Patria, Editorial Director; Rachel Lockhart, Commissioning Editor;
Anya Wilson, Managing Editor; Bianca Knights, Assistant Editor
Production Ken Ruskin, Head of Pre-press and Production;
James Rudge, Production Artworker
Sales and Marketing Deborah Jones, Head of Sales and Marketing
Advertising Tom Lee, Commercial Director
Managing Director Toby Trotman

Designed by XAB

British Library Cataloguing in Publication Data
A catalogue record for this book is available from the British Library

ISBN 0 85660 990 0

Typeset by Tradespools Publishing Solutions
Printed and bound in Great Britain by
Cromwell Press, Trowbridge, Wiltshire

CONTENTS:

'We all have different body shapes... we are all still very important and make a useful contribution to the world.'

REAL LIFE ISSUES:
Eating Disorders

ABOUT THE AUTHOR

Heather Warner's working life began as a schoolteacher in a rural seaside village in Trinidad before travelling to the UK to begin a career in health. She completed her mental health nurse training in 1995 at the University of North London in conjunction with the North London Joint College of Health Studies (now a faculty of the Middlesex University) and later on trained and qualified as a Systemic family and couple psychotherapist in 2002 at the Institute of Family Therapy, London. Specialising in eating disorders nursing since 1998, she is currently the service manager and a senior clinician at the Royal Free Eating Disorders Service, Camden and Islington Mental Health and Social Care NHS Trust.

REAL LIFE ISSUES:
Eating Disorders

ACKNOWLEDGEMENTS

Thank you to Zoe Chivers and other staff from CfBT Connexions Hounslow for their contributions to this book.

A special thank you to my husband, Jez Caudle, who was a fantastic source of encouragement and support.

INTRODUCTION

This book is about eating disorders and looks at how young people can be at risk from these conditions. An eating disorder is a very serious emotional problem and, if left untreated, could stay with you for a very long time – even for the rest of your life.

Reading this book will provide you with information about your body, how it is affected by the different eating disorders and the close link your body has with your emotions and your mind.

There are many problems associated with eating, but there are three eating disorders that we instantly recognise: anorexia nervosa, bulimia nervosa and binge eating disorder. This book will give a description of all of the emotional and physical problems associated with eating disorders and will also discuss in detail the three main eating disorders just mentioned, taking a look at the difficulties you could have if you suffer from one.

This book will also point you in the right direction to get more information and help for the very serious emotional and physical problems that occur as a result of having an eating disorder. Another aim of this book is to provide guidance to someone who might be concerned about a family member's or close friend's eating habits and weight loss or gain.

Knowledge is power! So, to know about such an issue, especially if you have some questions about your own experience of food and eating, is an important first step. With that in mind, I have included some very useful tips (Chapter 13), and the following glossary of terms explains all the words that may be new to you.

GLOSSARY OF TERMS

▪ **Amenorrhoea [A-MEN-OH-REE-AH]:** The absence of periods
▪ **Compensatory behaviours:** Things you might do to get rid of unwanted calories, which may involve forcing yourself to vomit, abusing laxatives, diuretics or enemas, exercising excessively and/or fasting
▪ **Diagnosis:** The name of a disease or condition
▪ **Diuretic:** A type of medication that gets rid of water from your body
▪ **Empathise:** Emotionally relate to another person
▪ **Faddy eating:** Developing a certain liking for only one or two food items, for example pasta or baked beans, and refusing to eat anything else
▪ **Food restriction:** Constantly eating far less than what is required to keep your weight the same
▪ **Hypokalaemia:** Having too little potassium in your body, which is very dangerous
▪ **Hypothalamus:** A gland in your brain that is linked to your nervous system and controls body temperature, hunger and thirst
▪ **Lanugo hair:** A fine downy layer of hair covering the body all over

- **Menarche [MEN-ARK-EE]:** Point at which a girl develops and is able to have periods. This is a sign she is able to get pregnant
- **Menopause:** The stage in a woman's life when she experiences a change in her hormones and after which she can no longer have children
- **Menstruation:** Periods
- **Metabolic rate:** The speed at which your body uses energy or burns calories
- **Metabolism:** The using up of energy by the body
- **Obsessive-compulsive disorder:** An illness where the person feels that they must do certain things in a certain way for fear of something terrible happening
- **Parotid glands:** Salivary glands
- **Phobia:** An irrational and uncontrollable fear of something
- **Poly Cystic Ovarian Syndrome (PCOS):** A very serious complication resulting in cysts or little balls being formed on your ovaries which can cause long-lasting difficulties with fertility and hormones
- **Psychological:** Mental or emotional in nature
- **Psychotherapy:** Treatment involving talking about your situation in a way that helps you to change your thoughts and emotions through a greater understanding of them
- **Russell marks:** Calluses or hard skin on knuckles caused from the wear and tear caused by using fingers to help bring about vomiting
- **Set point weight:** The weight to which your body will always want to return and at which you will feel and function at your best
- **Syndrome:** A collection of characteristics and health problems in an individual which usually has a single underlying cause; as well as a group of signs and symptoms that occur together and characterise a particular disease.

CHAPTER ONE:

WHAT IS AN EATING DISORDER?
What are eating disorders made of?

When someone has an eating disorder their eating can be affected in many ways. However, there are three types of eating disorders that are most popularly recognised.

ANOREXIA NERVOSA

One way an eating disorder can affect you is when you do not eat enough and as a result you lose weight to the point that your body eventually becomes unable to cope with the weight loss. The **diagnosis** given to this eating disorder is **anorexia nervosa**.

If the amount of food you eat works out to be much less than the amount of calories or energy you use up, the result is that you lose a significant amount of weight over time. But if you are someone with anorexia nervosa, the weight loss you achieve is something that makes

FACT BOX

Diagnosis: *the name of a disease or condition.*

you feel good about yourself and you would continue to try to lose weight even though your health might be poor as a result.

Even in the face of serious health problems and damage to your body, if you have anorexia nervosa, you would continue to eat much less than you need to be healthy, or even to stay alive. There is a range of problems that you can experience as a result of continuous weight loss, especially physical problems. Your vital organs such as the heart, kidneys, liver and brain become seriously damaged.

In Chapter 6 you will find much more about anorexia nervosa.

BULIMIA NERVOSA

Another way you can be affected by an eating disorder is when you think about food constantly and eat large quantities of food at once or binge. At the same time, you are constantly wishing to be thinner than you are.

This obsession with food and thinness usually means that you also spend a lot of time thinking about how to lose weight. These thoughts are accompanied by drastic methods or **compensatory behaviours** to lose weight, such as dieting, starving for significant periods of the day, exercising, leaving out certain food groups from your diet, vomiting and taking laxatives without having a need to. In moderation these actions can be relatively harmless, but it is the degree to which they are done that causes a problem.

If you suffer from **bulimia nervosa** your weight would likely be within the normal weight range or you would be slightly overweight. Chapter 8 discusses bulimia nervosa in more detail.

FACT BOX

Compensatory behaviours are things you might do to get rid of unwanted calories, and may involve forcing yourself to vomit, abusing laxatives, diuretics or enemas, exercising excessively and/or fasting.

BINGE EATING DISORDER

You can also be affected by an eating disorder in a way that makes you obsessed about food and binge, but without doing anything (i.e. not using the compensatory behaviours) to control your weight. As a result, your weight goes up and up, sometimes resulting in you becoming obese.

If you have this eating disorder, you may not be happy with your weight going up due to the bingeing, but you would not push yourself to lose weight in such drastic ways as someone who is suffering from bulimia nervosa. Therefore you would more than likely remain large in size. You would be suffering from **binge eating disorder**.

Chapter 9 takes an in-depth look into binge eating disorder.

AN EATING DISORDER NOT MENTIONED ABOVE

When people think of eating disorders, they usually think instantly about anorexia nervosa, bulimia nervosa or, less often, binge eating disorder. The fact is that the majority of eating disorders exist outside of these neat labels. It will be difficult to find people suffering from one distinct eating disorder. For example, someone who mainly eats very little so that they lose weight constantly, may also make themselves vomit. Also someone who binges along with doing the compensatory behaviours may still be obese. So it is better to view these three types of disorders known as **syndromes** as similar types of eating problems.

You may find that the eating problem someone is experiencing cannot be neatly slotted into any of the three diagnoses but has a mixture of two or more conditions. When this occurs the person will be suffering from an eating disorder that is not typical and therefore is called an **eating disorder not otherwise specified (EDNOS)** or an **atypical eating disorder**. These are discussed in detail in Chapter 10.

WHAT ARE EATING DISORDERS MADE OF?

Before we go into the detail of the various eating disorders, it is important to understand the main things that are going wrong when you suffer from an eating disorder.

FACT BOX

Syndrome: a collection of characteristics and health problems in an individual which usually has a single underlying cause; as well as a group of signs and symptoms that occur together and characterise a particular disease.

Within an eating disorder, the way that you eat and see food is a major part of what goes wrong and sometimes it is easy to stumble into an eating disorder simply because of how you happen to be eating at the time. When we are growing up it is common to experiment with eating – do you remember being told not to play with your food? Particularly when we are younger, strange eating habits can happen, often out of boredom, curiosity or to get away from eating a particular food we hate.

However, that perfectly innocent, but *weird* attitude to food and eating at a certain point in your life can lead you to continue eating in that same way, which might trigger a way of thinking about your **body** and **weight**. Experts believe that, over time, if you have problems with your emotional well-being, these habits can lead to an eating disorder. Before you know it, you can get caught in a destructive pattern of eating very little, or eating too much then getting rid of the food or just eating too much.

The next four chapters explain important information about:
- Eating
- Your body
- Your mind
- Being different.

For you to have a greater understanding of eating disorders, these chapters are very important, so make sure you read on!

CHAPTER TWO:

EATING AND THE BODY
Why do we get hungry?

Eating is one of the first things we learn to do from the time we are born. It is the key to staying alive and through our evolution our bodies have become efficient so that we could survive the most difficult situations, particularly famine.

HUNGER AND SATISFACTION

Hunger tells our bodies to look for food and **satisfaction** stops us from eating further; they don't start in our stomachs but in our brains in a place called the **hypothalamus**. The hypothalamus works closely with the amount of sugar in our blood to help create the feelings of hunger and satisfaction. Blood-sugar levels increase after we eat something and get very low when we need to eat.

FACT BOX

*The **hypothalamus** is a gland in your brain that is linked to your nervous system and controls body temperature, **hunger** and thirst.*

How the hypothalamus is related to the eating process is shown in the diagram below.

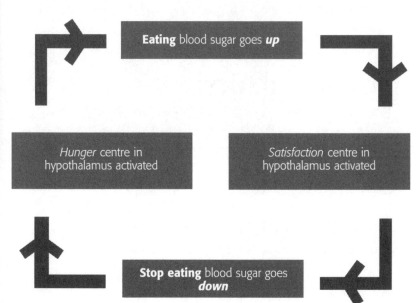

Eating blood sugar goes *up*

Hunger centre in hypothalamus activated

Satisfaction centre in hypothalamus activated

Stop eating blood sugar goes *down*

HOW THE HYPOTHALAMUS IS RELATED TO EATING AND THE FEELINGS OF HUNGER AND SATISFACTION.

Having any type of eating disorder causes confusion in the hypothalamus and so you can lose the ability to know when you are hungry or satisfied after eating and this can lead to serious problems. The good news is that this damage can be put right in time.

FOOD AS ENERGY

The hypothalamus is extremely important because eating is essential for us. There are a lot of processes that go on inside us just to keep our bodies fit and healthy enough to produce children. Eating is the way of getting fuel into the body in order to be able to carry out these processes. Think of your body as a car – you need to put petrol in the tank for a car to work and it is the same with food for your body. Your body breaks down the food and converts it into energy that can power the different parts of the body.

FOOD GROUPS

There's a well-known phrase, 'You are what you eat'. It's true. What and how you eat can reflect the way you feel and cope with what life throws at you. There are four groups of food that you should have in varying amounts in your diet. For a balanced diet you need to eat a variety of foods from all four groups.

Bread, cereal, rice and pasta

Bread, cereal, rice, and pasta are all great sources of **carbohydrates**, the nutrient that is the body's major energy provider. So if you're very active and need lots of energy, make sure you eat plenty of carbohydrates. It should form the main part of your daily meals, with five or more servings per day.

Fruits and vegetables

Vegetables are great because they are packed full of **vitamins and minerals**, which are needed to keep your skin, bones and teeth healthy. Carrots are a good source of Vitamin A, and tomatoes are great for Vitamin C.

Fruits are fantastic because not only do they taste great but they also provide important vitamins that keep you feeling fine and looking good. You will find a lot of Vitamin C in fruits like oranges and strawberries. Fruits also supply carbohydrates, the body's favourite kind of fuel, and are full of fibre, which helps in your digestion. You should aim for five daily servings of fruit and vegetables for a healthy balanced diet. Choose dark green and orange vegetables and orange fruit more often as they have the most nutrients.

Meat, poultry, fish, beans, eggs and nuts

Meat, chicken, fish, beans, eggs and nuts are all a very good source of **protein**. Protein is very important as it forms the building blocks of cells, it can help your body grow and repair itself. They also provide important minerals such as iron and zinc. You should aim for two or three servings per day of food from this group.

Milk, yoghurt and cheese

Eating and drinking milk, yoghurt and cheese is the best way to get your daily calcium, which is essential for healthy bones and teeth. There is plenty of protein in this food group. These foods are very important for good health, and you should have two to four servings per day.

LIQUIDS

Liquids are not a food group, but are essential to our bodies working properly. We are constantly losing water through normal exercise and everyday activity. It is recommended that we drink approximately two litres of water per day. You can get liquids from **water, juices, tea, coffee** and foods such as **celery, lettuce** and **oranges.**

FATS, OILS AND SWEETS

Fats, oils and sweets are also not part of a food group as such. Fat is very important as it helps in the production of new cell membranes and certain hormones in the body, as well as providing the protective padding for bones and internal organs. Fat is a concentrated source of energy, and foods that are high in fat provide a lot of energy. In today's world it is easy to consume too much energy (calories) when eating a high fat diet. If you take in more energy than you use through exercising, growing and everyday activity, then the **excess energy** is stored in the body as fat, and this could lead to you becoming overweight or obese. Our bodies are designed this way because at one time we needed to be able to store energy because food was so scarce.

Your body needs fat, but you need to make sure you have the *right kind* of fats and oils. Lean meat, and fish such as salmon, provide 'good fat'. Vegetable oils such as olive oil are very good for you, whereas too much animal fat such as butter can be bad for your heart. And although sugary foods like chocolate and biscuits are carbohydrates and can give you an energy boost, they're usually full of calories and don't offer much in the way of nutrients. Eat only a little bit of these foods and don't eat them very often.

Health experts have studied the amounts of major food groups that you need each day. As a rough guide, here is a range of the amounts of each group of nutrients that is required.

FOOD GROUPS	AMOUNT PER DAY
Liquids	2 litres daily
Breads and Cereals	About 40% of diet
Vegetable and fruit	Apprx 30% of diet
Protein and healthy fats	Apprx 20% of diet
Fats	Very little, about 10% of diet

Dietary Reference Guide

Everyone is different and what you need in your daily diet may be different to what your best friend needs. For example, if you're on the running team at school you would need a higher energy-based diet than someone whose main extra curricular activity is playing chess.

FOOD AND OUR EMOTIONS

Because eating is so important, our emotions are closely related to it. Ever noticed how the thought of your favourite food can give you a pleasant feeling? Or when your dinnertime gets delayed because you are stuck on a bus on your way home from school in a traffic jam, this sometimes makes you cross?

As a teenager, you will be going through a very emotional stage mainly because you are starting to do things independently for the first time and you will definitely get things wrong. Trial and error is probably one of the best ways of learning, but at a time when you are going through physical as well as emotional changes, getting something wrong can be very stressful, and you may end up thinking perhaps you can't do anything at all.

There is a close link between how we feel emotionally and our need or desire for food. Even the way we talk about our emotions can be similar to the language we use to talk about food: 'you're full of beans' is a way of saying someone is cheerful or full of energy. The opposite is true as well, in that sometimes when we feel sad either we don't feel like eating or we have one of our favourite foods to make us feel better. When this link becomes so strong that our ability to feed ourselves is taken over *totally* by the way we feel or would like to feel to the point that we cannot function normally, then we have developed an eating disorder.

CHAPTER THREE:

MY BODY; EVERY BODY'S DIFFERENT
Useful ways to describe our bodies

WEIGHT RANGES

An eating disorder is an emotional problem that results in a change in your body as you try to regulate your weight and how you look. So, it is important to have an idea of what is considered to be a healthy weight range. The **body mass index** (BMI) is a measure of your weight to height ratio which was developed by scientists to find out at what weights the human body is at its healthiest and at what weights the body is most at risk from certain diseases. The BMI is your weight in kilograms divided by the square of your height in metres. It is very easy to calculate. Here is an example:

Weight = 59.7 kg

Height = 1.67 m

Multiply the value of your height by itself then you get your **height squared**:

Height squared = 1.67 m × 1.67 m = 2.79 m^2

Now divide your weight by your height squared:

Weight/height squared = 59.7 kg/2.79 m^2

BMI = 21.4

So, within every 1 square metre of your body, there are 21.4 kg of weight in that space; this is your mass per square metre.

Now calculate your own BMI. For this you will need a calculator.

My weight =_____

My height =_____

My height squared =_____

My weight/height squared = _____

My BMI =_____

If you only know your weight and height in feet and inches and in stones and pounds, then do the following calculations:
- Divide your weight in pounds by 2.21; this is your weight in kilograms, then
- Divide your height in inches by 39.4; this is your height in metres, and
- Use your weight in kilograms and your height in metres in the BMI calculations above.

By calculating your BMI you will know whether you are in a healthy weight range or not. BMI is very important as it can indicate what diseases a person is prone to.

BMI ranges with related illnesses and conditions

If your body mass index (BMI) is:

■ Less than 12 it means you are at a life-threatening **anorexic** weight

■ Less than 17.5 it means you are within the **anorexic** weight range, resulting in amenorrhoea (no periods); you begin to lose cells from all your body organs; you begin to suffer problems with your bones, heart, muscle and brain

■ Between 17.5 and 20 it means you are **underweight** and, for girls, you may have irregular or absent periods

■ Between 20 and 25 it means you are within the **normal** weight range

■ Between 25 and 30 it means you are in the **overweight** weight range

■ More than 30 it means you are in the **obese** weight range and at risk of diabetes. All your organs are at risk of serious damage – your bones, heart, muscle and brain

■ More than 40 it means you are **morbidly (severely) obese**.

BMI is a measure calculated mostly for people aged 14 or more. If you are younger than 14, a doctor or nurse can see if you are in the normal weight range by comparing your weight and height to a special chart for young people.

SET POINT WEIGHT

The different BMIs indicate our physical health. If you've ever been on a diet or if you've fallen ill, you may have lost a few pounds. And when that happens you might have felt weak or 'not yourself' for a while. This is because each of us has a particular weight at which we operate best, and falling below or going above that weight makes us feel out of sorts. The weight at which our bodies feel most comfortable is called our **set point weight** and your body always wants to return to this weight.

Your set point weight is influenced by your genetics (what you have inherited from your family), the things and amount you eat, and what you did at important developmental stages in your life as a:

- baby
- young child
- pre-teenager (9–12 years)
- young adult (17–19 years).

For girls, when you grow older, what you do while you are pregnant or later during your **menopause** can also influence your set point weight.

BODY SHAPES

Similar to your set point weight, your body shape is determined by your genetics and what you did at important growing and developmental stages in your life (the same stages as for the set weight point). For girls, when you grow older, what you do while you

FACT BOX

Menopause is the stage in a woman's life when she experiences a change in her hormones and after which she can no longer have children.

are pregnant or later during your menopause can also influence your set body shape.

Depending on what you read you will see body shapes categorised in one of two ways. The more traditional way divides body shapes into **apples**, **pears** and **slender** and tends to be used when talking about female body shapes. These are quite helpful because the fruits chosen actually reflect the shape the body takes on and it makes it easy to remember which is which. We get our shapes from how the fat and muscle place themselves around our skeleton.

Apples

In apple shapes, fat tends to be deposited mainly around your middle, above and around the waist, where your heart and other major organs are situated. Therefore, apple shapes tend to have a lower waist to hip ratio – that is, their waists are not that much smaller than their hips. People with this body shape are susceptible to heart disease, particularly if they are overweight. Apple-shaped stars are Liv Tyler, Meera Syal and Emma Bunton.

Pears

In pear shapes, the fat tends to settle around your hips and thighs, or below your waist. Therefore pear shapes are more likely to have a higher waist to hip ratio (their waists are much smaller than their hips) and are less susceptible to heart disease. Even though pear shapes have a lower risk of heart disease, any gain in weight tends to go straight on to your hips and thighs, which most people, particularly women, are not happy about. Examples of pear-shaped stars are Beyonce Knowles and Davina McCall.

Slender

Slender, straight or tubular-shaped people tend to struggle to put on weight as fat barely has time to stay because of their high **metabolic rate**. This tends to be the most sought-after shape and the most difficult to attain. Slender-shaped stars are Naomi Campbell and Nicole Kidman.

FACT BOX	***Metabolism*** *is the using up of energy by the body. Therefore your* ***metabolic rate*** *is the speed at which your body uses energy or burns calories.*

Soma types

The less traditional way of grouping the types of body shapes looks at **soma types**, developed by William H. Sheldon in 1940 (www.time-to-run.com/physiology/bodytype.htm). They are as follows:

- ■ Ectomorph – small-framed and slender in shape
- ■ Endomorph – round and 'big boned' in build
- ■ Mesomorph – muscular build, wide shoulders and slim waist.

Examples of ectomorph body shapes are Kate Moss and Jennifer Aniston; of endomorphs are Oprah Winfrey and Johnny Vegas; and of mesomorphs are Tom Cruise and Nell McAndrew.

EVERY BODY'S DIFFERENT

The weights and shapes looked at in these chapters are by no means perfect and in fact have been criticised because they can't describe *all* human shapes and forms. Don't be worried if you are struggling to find a category that your body shape fits into. We all have different body shapes, which means that we all look different and may struggle a lot to look like someone who has a different body shape to ours. However, despite their imperfections, these ways of categorising weights and shapes are still very useful in helping us think of our bodies. It is a bit like us really, although no body's perfect, we are all still very important and make a useful contribution to the world.

MIND AND BODY
Changes you might experience

As a teenager, you experience one of the most adventurous times of your life, mainly because you begin to experiment and do things on your own for the first time. Going out with friends, shopping, dating, choosing your career and going travelling are some of the things you get to do with no adults around. You can really enjoy this time of life but not without a few hard times and rejections along the way. When you really think about it, you need to be fit and healthy to handle what life throws your way during this time. The first step to becoming fighting fit is your body. How you look on the outside, how you feel on the inside and your attitude to eating can help or hurt your efforts to get through your teenage years.

MENTAL HEALTH

When we talk about a person's mental health we mean their emotional well-being. Some of the things that contribute to emotional well-being are:

- Having good self-esteem
- A supportive family home
- Parents who get on, even when separated or divorced

- Being able to form long-lasting relationships with friends and family
- Being independent
- Being able to look forward to and be curious about new experiences
- Reliable and safe support in the community outside of home
- Having a healthy, happy imagination and some creativity when dealing with difficulty
- Ability to be aware of others' feelings and experiences and **empathise** with them
- Being able to experience **psychological** pain and learn from the experience after getting over it, thus making your life richer.

FACT BOX

Empathise: emotionally relate to another person.
Psychological: mental or emotional in nature.

When one or more of the contributing factors to emotional well-being are missing, there is a chance that you can experience emotional issues that can result in mental health difficulties. An eating disorder is a problem that occurs as a result of someone having mental health problems, and can start to take root during your teenage years or before.

Even with all the positive factors in place, however, emotional problems can occur as a result of a direct stress that can happen when going from one stage of life to the next. Therefore, for many reasons, growing up can be a bit daunting and full of normal pressures such as:
- exams
- moving house

- going to a new school
- starting university
- leaving home
- first relationships.

> **For a closer look at dealing with these issues, see other books in the *Real Life Issues* series *Stress, Coping with Life* and *Sex and Relationships*.**

You might also experience some pressures on top of the normal ones. These could be:

- being bullied
- your parents splitting up
- remembering physical or sexual abuse you suffered in the past (or are still suffering)
- being in a relationship you feel unable to stop or get out of
- missing home after fleeing your country due to war and persecution
- someone close to you discovering they have a severe and incurable illness
- living with a parent or older brother/sister who has mental health difficulties themselves
- a close friend or relative dying.

These pressures can be quite damaging, especially on top of everyday teenage trouble. Having to deal with one or more of these pressures can result in you feeling unable to do the simplest of tasks. Some mental health problems experienced by teenagers and young adults are:

- Having an uncontrollable urge to perform a task repeatedly, when there is no need to do so, for fear of something very bad happening. This is called **obsessive-compulsive disorder**.

■ Always feeling sad and low, resulting in poor personal hygiene, always being moody and irritable, lacking an interest in keeping your surroundings clean, not enjoying anything and, in extreme cases, not wanting to live. This is called **depression**.

■ Going through extreme phases of feeling on top of the world one minute to feeling down in the dumps the next, breaking the rules at school, not having much time for anyone in authority and feeling extremely guilty after acts of extreme rebellion. Swinging from these emotional highs and lows to the point that you are unable to be yourself or do 'normal' things are symptoms of **manic depression** or **bipolar disorder**.

■ Inflicting harm on yourself, mainly cutting or burning your skin as a sign of turmoil and distress. This is called **self-harm**.

■ Being confused by intrusive thoughts you have, which sometimes relate to other people or yourself, resulting in you feeling in danger or at risk of harm. Your senses and perceptions of what is real are often disturbed. Experiencing such extreme confusion about what is real can cause intense emotional distress and even make you feel more and more out of touch with reality. This is called **schizophrenia**.

■ Experiencing a disturbance to your eating, with you either eating too little or too much food sometimes alongside a range of efforts to lose weight in other ways so that you can control or cope with emotional turmoil. This is called an **eating disorder**.

BODY IMAGE

Remember in Chapter 2 when we talked about how closely our bodies and our minds work together? Well, we always have our bodies in mind. In our minds we hold an **image** of our body and can fairly accurately estimate whether we are tall or short, big or small, usually by looking at how we are compared to other people around us. Our peer group acts as a guide to what is a normal size for us at our age, for our sex and for our race.

There are many ways to think of our body and have an image of it. Our body image is formed by our view of parts of ourselves including the following:

- weight
- size
- shape
- body hygiene
- sense of style
- physical abilities: to walk; to see; to hear; to speak
- hair colour
- hair texture
- eye colour
- skin colour
- posture.

Because during your teenage years your body changes so much, how you feel about it can change from time to time. It's also quite a hectic time in your life and you can have a very busy social life. If this is the case, you may have enough distractions to stop yourself getting too caught up with yourself. However, for some, this just does not happen and constantly thinking about your body can have a bad effect, causing your mind to play tricks on you, to give you a **distorted** view of your body, or just make you down on yourself, making you **dissatisfied** with your body.

DISTORTED BODY IMAGE

Always thinking about, looking at, touching or checking your body because you think you are too big, too short, etc. can lead to the image you have of yourself becoming distorted. For example, you can think of your body image only in terms of weight and become focused on actions and behaviour to constantly adjust it to what you think is perfect. When this happens you have what is called a **distorted body image**. There are many different things you have to think about when it comes to your body, and so focusing on one aspect of your body can make you forget all the other bits that make up your body image. Someone suffering from an eating disorder can have this problem.

BODY DISSATISFACTION

When you feel that bits of yourself are not up to scratch or you feel that your body is inadequate, then you may be suffering from a poor body image. Having a **low body satisfaction** can lead you to using drastic measures to get your body the way you want it. Someone suffering from an eating disorder can have this problem. The trouble is, if your self-esteem is too low, you will never be satisfied no matter how much your body changes as a result of the things you do to your weight or shape.

> **For a closer look at self-esteem, see *Real Life Issues: Confidence and Self-esteem*.**

BODY SATISFACTION

There is a certain level of security that comes with looking like everyone else. Because humans are social animals, we feel a sense of belonging when we are similar to those around us. You can say this is a basic link between how we look and how we feel. This link means

that for every country or culture, there are certain expectations or
cultural norms of how you should look.

Here is a questionnaire designed to look at body satisfaction.

Questionnaire about body satisfaction

To answer the questions, indicate whether you strongly disagree,
disagree, are neutral, agree or strongly agree by ticking in the
appropriate box.

Once you have finished, add up your score and see what that means
about your body satisfaction. Just remember there are no right or
wrong answers and the questions are not meant to trick you!

---

1 I *always* think my stomach is too big

STRONGLY DISAGREE	DISAGREE	NEUTRAL	AGREE	STRONGLY AGREE
1	2	3	4	5
☐	☐	☐	☐	☐

2 I *always* think my thighs are too large

STRONGLY DISAGREE	DISAGREE	NEUTRAL	AGREE	STRONGLY AGREE
1	2	3	4	5
☐	☐	☐	☐	☐

3 I am terrified of gaining weight

STRONGLY DISAGREE	DISAGREE	NEUTRAL	AGREE	STRONGLY AGREE
1	2	3	4	5
☐	☐	☐	☐	☐

4 I am *never* satisfied with the shape of my body

STRONGLY DISAGREE	DISAGREE	NEUTRAL	AGREE	STRONGLY AGREE
1	2	3	4	5
☐	☐	☐	☐	☐

5 I *always* make a huge fuss about the importance of my weight

STRONGLY DISAGREE	DISAGREE	NEUTRAL	AGREE	STRONGLY AGREE
1	2	3	4	5
☐	☐	☐	☐	☐

6 I hate the shape of my buttocks

STRONGLY DISAGREE	DISAGREE	NEUTRAL	AGREE	STRONGLY AGREE
1	2	3	4	5
☐	☐	☐	☐	☐

7 I *always* think my hips are too big

STRONGLY DISAGREE	DISAGREE	NEUTRAL	AGREE	STRONGLY AGREE
1	2	3	4	5
☐	☐	☐	☐	☐

8 I *always* think my arms are too big

STRONGLY DISAGREE	DISAGREE	NEUTRAL	AGREE	STRONGLY AGREE
1	2	3	4	5
☐	☐	☐	☐	☐

9 There is *always* someone around whose body I prefer to my own

STRONGLY DISAGREE	DISAGREE	NEUTRAL	AGREE	STRONGLY AGREE
1	2	3	4	5
☐	☐	☐	☐	☐

Results

9–18: If your score is within this range then you have very high body satisfaction. You are completely satisfied with your body and you may believe that you are as close to perfection as is humanly possible. This may be due to the fact that you work very hard to keep your body in the shape you prefer or simply that the way people look is just not that important to you so you love yourself no matter how you look. This questionnaire is about attitude and this score says that you love what you have, and this is great. The only thing I would watch out for is valuing your 'perfect looks' above other things such as your inner talents or the love of your friends and family. Because your body is something that changes, if you place too high a value on your perfect looks now, it may be quite distressing if you lose that perfection.

19–27: If your score is within this range, then you have a moderate to high body satisfaction. Your view of what you look like is balanced and you seem to have embraced your body – even the parts that are not perfect. If you have identified things that you are not satisfied with, your balanced view means that you are in charge of how you feel about them. My guess is that, if you thought about something you are not completely satisfied with, you would do something that is not damaging to how you value yourself. By that I mean you would probably think about pampering your body with something relaxing or energising, not because you want to lose weight or change anything, but because it will make you feel relaxed and good about yourself.

28–36: If your score is within this range it means you have a moderate to low body satisfaction, possibly to the point that you have started thinking about ways to change your body. You are in the group that is most likely to start dieting and/or extreme gym or exercise regimes. This is not an advisable way to solve your body dissatisfaction because dieting can lead to you eating below what you require, thus lowering your energy levels and your metabolism and making you feel lethargic. Thinking about what we discussed in Chapter 2, reducing your food intake would cause your body to go into 'hunt food' mode and increase the chance of you breaking your diet. This could lead to you **yo-yo dieting**, that is starting a new diet, stopping the diet so your weight goes up, then starting another new diet, and so on, resulting in your weight going up and down. You are still capable of appreciating a small part of yourself, but you struggle to keep hold of that. Watch out for disliking your body even more and start talking to others whom you trust and love about what you think.

37–45: If your score is within this range this means you have a very low body satisfaction, possibly to the point that you have developed or are developing an eating disorder due to your efforts to change your body. You may be thinking about, or have even already tried ways to lose weight or change the size and shape of a particular body part. The danger with this is that you might be dissatisfied not only with your weight, but also with other things that might be taking place in your life. Such a strong dissatisfaction with your body may mean that your self-esteem is very low or you are going through something very difficult, which you believe you have to sort out all on your own. Such a high score could be because you are being (or have been) bullied or ridiculed as a result of your weight and therefore are finding it difficult to see anything positive about your self.

CASE STUDY

Emma never felt she fitted in being a tall girl in school and as a result always felt awkward and different from everyone else. After a while this made her feel that there was something wrong with her and she got very depressed. Emma's emotional well-being was affected by the fact that at home she was always being told about her mistakes, which gave her the impression she never got anything right. Her father insisted on her becoming a doctor when all she wanted to do was be an artist and although she tried to follow her dream, she never felt that what she was doing was approved of and this affected how she felt about herself.

At the age of 14, Emma hated eating and thought that food was disgusting to the point that, although she would eat very little, she

s. She
and out as
tand her body
ich hung out
ll went down
use taking so
d to affect her
blood that

tarted seeing
her body

eels like
ing
to get
ting and
ling. I
like
oliath'
e boys
like this,
e. If I
but

Emma

A way of lea

Being happy with yourself

The easiest way to start is

you like the best, or in som

things you like about that

your second-best (or seco

you get to parts that are r

to see the good things in t

impossible or even silly, bu

satisfied with your body.

SELF-EST

Our self-esteem is the valu

important to our emotiona

physically throughout life,

nurturing and taking care

In the same as way our ph

give us nutrition that can r

health, similarly our emotic

and negative comments c

either high self-esteem or

emotionally based, it is no

about us that have an imp

comments are said and h

impact on our self-esteem

damage self-esteem and

things independently.

For more on se

Confid

frequently vomited up the food she ate and took laxatives. She thought that if she lost enough weight, she would not stand out as much and people would not notice her. She could not stand her body and felt that no one liked her in school so she pretty much hung out on her own. As she grew older, it got worse and her BMI went down to 16. She needed to go into hospital a few times because taking so many laxatives and vomiting whilst eating so little started to affect her heart, because of her low potassium (a chemical in the blood that helps your heart to work).

Emma eventually asked her family doctor for help and started seeing a therapist. She often talked about how much she hated her body and was totally dissatisfied with it.

Honestly, when I have a meal it feels like a carrier bag full of sick is swimming around in my stomach and I have to get rid of it. I feel horrible and disgusting and always want to get rid of that feeling. I always feel huge and my legs are like two huge tree trunks. I felt like 'Goliath' all the time in school and all of the boys used to make fun of me. At least like this, no one can say things that hurt me. If I keep to myself, it's easier – lonely, but safer.

Emma

A way of learning to love yourself!

Being happy with yourself is something that you have to learn to do. The easiest way to start is to think about the part of your body that you like the best, or in some cases, hate the least and write down all things you like about that part. Do this for 5–10 days then move on to your second-best (or second-least worst) part and repeat. The closer you get to parts that are really difficult for you, take a longer time trying to see the good things in them, no matter how tiny. This may seem impossible or even silly, but it is an important start to learning to be satisfied with your body.

SELF-ESTEEM

Our self-esteem is the value we place on ourselves and is very important to our emotional make up. Just as we feed our bodies physically throughout life, so too is our emotional self in need of nurturing and taking care of.

In the same as way our physical body is fed by food and liquids, which give us nutrition that can result in us having either good health or bad health, similarly our emotional self is fed positive comments (praise) and negative comments (criticism), which can result in us having either high self-esteem or low self-esteem. Because self-esteem is so emotionally based, it is not simply the types of comments that are said about us that have an impact, but it is also the *way* that the comments are said and *how many* are said that can have a significant impact on our self-esteem. Using critical comments too much can damage self-esteem and even stop people from being able to do things independently.

> **For more on self-esteem, see *Real Life Issues:***
> ***Confidence and Self-esteem.***

SELF-WORTH

Self-worth is the amount of importance we place on ourselves and what contribution we can make to the world and the people around us. This is something that is hard to measure, but we are all able to estimate whether we believe we are important or can make a difference to what goes on around us.

As a teenager, there are times when you may feel low about how your life is going, mainly as you try to make sense of it. One thing that makes your life worthwhile is the fact that you are part of something to which you make a contribution, be it school and the fact that you have friends who enjoy your company, or a club where your activities, together with those of the other club members, are very important for the club's survival. Perhaps in your family you have a very important position as the eldest girl, the youngest child, a foster brother, the middle child or a stepsister – something that makes you quite special.

This position of importance can be stressful yet fulfilling because you mean a lot to many people. If you are unable to recognise this or for some reason you underestimate your importance to your friends and family, you may be suffering from a **low self-worth**.

Your self-worth is affected by your:
- Relationships with family and friends
- Achievements
- Ability to communicate with others
- Self-esteem.

'WHAT ABOUT MY BODY?'

So far you have been reading about the types of eating disorders and you have learned important information about our bodies, the links between the way we eat and our feelings, and ways to describe the shape and size of our bodies. If you are thinking to yourself 'what about my body? I'm not really comfortable with it – what does this mean?', then the next chapter will be of help to you. We will be looking more closely at how, as a teenager, it can be very difficult to figure out our bodies and the issues we or a close friend or relative of ours may be struggling with.

CHAPTER FIVE:

WE'RE ALL INDIVIDUALS!
In all shapes and sizes

In the previous chapters we looked at how diverse our bodies can be in terms of how tall and wide you are – body mass; how heavy you are – weight; and what kind of shape you are – body shape; as well as the body's connection to our minds. Scientists have studied all these things to get a better idea of how we function in order to keep our bodies fit and healthy, but we still don't know everything. One of the things you will realise after reading this book is that the cause of some eating disorders is still a bit of a mystery but huge efforts have gone into – and are still going into – finding ways of helping people who develop eating disorders, to lead a safe and normal life. The main reason for the mystery around the exact cause of an eating disorder is that we are all so different!

AGE

An eating disorder tends to start when you are beginning to take charge of your own body, generally when it is time for your control to change or to increase. The older we get the more responsibility we take on in looking after our bodies, and for some this responsibility creates anxiety, perhaps making you try harder and harder to be the healthiest you can be. Sometimes the pursuit of health takes over your life and the normal fears and concerns you can have as a teenager make you feel bad about yourself, leading you to do things which, in some cases, can develop into an eating disorder.

Look at the following table, which describes the different stages teenagers go through in life and what you usually have to do to successfully move on.

TRANSITION POINTS THROUGH THE TEENAGE YEARS STAGE	MAIN SOCIAL AND PSYCHOLOGICAL CONCERNS	ISSUES TO WORK THROUGH
12–14 years old (early stage of adolescence)	Dealing with the dramatic physical changes that you are going through as a result of puberty. Your body is changing shape and this is stressful.	▪ If you are a girl you might be concerned with maturing too early, being overweight, being too tall, and not being thought of as attractive to boys. ▪ If you are a boy, on the other hand, the sooner you mature the better, you might not want to be too small or too short or not strong enough. You are starting to take risks in separating from the security of your family and you are thinking of forming relationships with others.
14–16 years old (middle stage of adolescence)	Making relationships with your peers. You are beginning to think more about yourself and the world, and you use your thoughts	▪ Dating starts in this phase and you begin exploring your sexual experiences as well as sexual orientation (whether you are gay or straight).

TRANSITION POINTS THROUGH THE TEENAGE YEARS STAGE	MAIN SOCIAL AND PSYCHOLOGICAL CONCERNS	ISSUES TO WORK THROUGH
	to increasingly distance yourself from your parents. 'Most grown ups are "rubbish" and it's better all round if you stick to your mates.'	■ As a result you are beginning to experience difficult emotions more often, such as: anger, guilt, fear of being abandoned, rebellion. ■ It's natural for many of your relationships to fail and so you learn to handle rejection in this stage.
16–19 years old (late stage of adolescence)	Your energies are divided mainly into what career you would like to pursue and how to form intimate romantic relationships.	■ Job interviews, university interviews and, in some cases, meeting new flatmates or housemates before you move into new accommodation, take up a lot of your time. ■ It dawns on you that your future is in your hands and you have to do things mainly yourself or with someone who is going to be with you for the rest of your life. ■ As a result your interpersonal relationships become deeper and more meaningful as you start to get practice in making long-term commitments to your friends and that special someone you share a sexual intimacy with.

TRANSITION POINTS THROUGH THE TEENAGE YEARS STAGE	MAIN SOCIAL AND PSYCHOLOGICAL CONCERNS	ISSUES TO WORK THROUGH
		▨ You will find you start drawing on the way your family used to do things, with the possibility of repeating both the good and bad things that went on as you grew up.

OUR ENVIRONMENT

As a country becomes wealthier, it becomes more successful at producing food. So, when you live in a country where food is abundant, such as the UK, being able to obtain food may not impress many people. In fact, in the face of such abundance, the ability to restrain from eating and have some 'self-control' and then show evidence of this by being thin can be seen even as a great achievement and can therefore be highly valued. For example, in Europe and America, being thin is a good thing.

As a result, in such 'modern' countries, eating disorders such as anorexia nervosa, bulimia nervosa and binge eating disorder are some of the conditions people suffer from as our survival instincts become confused by the amount of food there is around us. The world was once a place when food was a precious resource so we needed to be good at getting it. Now, in a modern world, where food is abundant, we have survival skills that are not always needed.

CULTURAL DIFFERENCES

In countries where food is still very scarce, the value placed on showing how well you can get and store food is crucial to your self-esteem and importance. In most African as well as Caribbean countries, it is normal to have a lot of curves or to 'have some fat on your bones'. In some non-western cultures such as those in China, Japan and Hong Kong, most people are of a shorter height than those in the western cultures and so this shorter height is considered normal. Cultures within India, Pakistan and Bangladesh are also used to smaller body frames, however, because of the amount of poverty there, a lot of importance may be placed on how well you can feed yourself and your family.

GENDER IDENTITY

Being a teenager growing up has its pressures; one of the main ones is forming your identity. Who we are as men and women is very important and even as babies we get messages about what it means to be a girl or a boy. I'm sure you've noticed that, for babies' clothes, pink is used for girls and blue for boys. In the same way, girls are more likely to get certain toys such as dolls or tea sets and boys would more likely get toy cars or adventure games. Playing with toys is great fun, but it also teaches us certain things about life and what can be expected of us. You can get quite a few good hints about how you should behave as a girl or a boy in our society through the examples we have in our families and in the media.

Sometimes, because of how we are on the inside it is difficult to follow the examples around us because we are different from what we are being asked to be like. For some parents, allowing their children to be themselves is a doddle! So if their daughter is a bit of a tomboy or their son likes playing with dolls and tea sets, they find it easy to allow their children to express themselves in the way they want to. Other parents, however, sometimes struggle and get anxious if their son or daughter does not behave 'normally'.

No matter how parents try to hide this anxiety, sometimes it can get passed on to their child who might receive the message that there is something wrong with them.

SEXUALITY

It's normal when growing up to be confused about how we feel about things. If you couldn't talk openly about your feelings as a child, then it is likely that you could enter your teenage years thinking that you'll never be able to talk about how you feel about your sexuality and so it becomes something that you might be ashamed of and so you think bad things about yourself. The feelings you start to experience as a teenager can feel threatening and so you might wish to stop your body developing. Doing this might be a way of you avoiding the pain of growing up into something you don't want to be.

FACT BOX

You are more likely as a young child to accurately identify emotions from facial expressions than you are as a teenager! Then it improves again when you become an adult.

An eating disorder, particularly anorexia nervosa, is a way of stopping the body from developing. The development that happens as a teenager is about becoming men and women. Girls get their periods (menstruate) and boys produce sperm, signalling the beginning of their sexual activity.

You may look around in society and try to find a role model but feel unable to reach the standards (which can be unrealistic) set by celebrities and sports stars. You may begin to obsess about ways to change how your body looks.

FOR BOYS WITH AN EATING DISORDER

It's not only girls and women who suffer from eating disorders. In England there are approximately 15,000 girls and women, and about 1,500 boys and men, who suffer from an eating disorder. For boys, eating difficulties and problems with eating can start much earlier than in girls in the form of **faddy eating**. This is when you develop a certain liking for only one or two food items (for example pasta or baked beans) and refuse to eat anything else. Another eating disorder that boys are more likely to suffer from than girls is **bigorexia** or **muscle dysmorphia**, discussed in more detail in Chapter 10.

Boys with an eating disorder can find it more difficult than girls to get help. Some reasons you may find it difficult as a boy to share your pain when you have an eating disorder are:
■ People only expect girls to suffer with an eating disorder
■ It is not 'normal' for boys to cry or show sadness
■ You might be afraid of being laughed at.

The dangerous thing about being afraid of talking to someone about your experience is that you wait until things are really bad before getting help. Most of the men who try to get help for an eating disorder do so when things get really bad and can suffer a lot of physical and emotional damage as a result.

CASE STUDY

Ephraim suffered from anorexia nervosa throughout his teens. When he first went to his family doctor at the age of 16 to get help he was told that boys do not suffer from anorexia nervosa and that he was dieting just a little too much. This sent him into despair and he did not go back to his doctor again until he was 19. He felt helpless as to how to start eating normally again and to work out the reasons he felt such a strong urge to control his food. Ephraim's anorexia started when, at the age of about 13, someone made a comment about his 'baby fat'. Upon hearing this comment he felt ugly and fat and intensely angry with this person for saying this. He had always felt self-conscious about his weight and was concerned that, as a boy, he was not muscular. He started to cut out all the fat from his diet and had only two meals a day. His became more and more obsessed with what he ate and even insisted on buying certain foods at certain places. He also exercised daily for several hours to the point that he hardly saw his friends anymore.

Ephraim's aim was to lose the 'baby fat', gain some muscle and look fit to show the person who made the comment when he was younger that he was muscular and attractive. What happened instead was that Ephraim became more and more obsessed with his food and exercise and nothing else. He started to lose touch with his friends. Life with his family started to suffer as well, as he became more and more irritable at home. Life at home started to revolve around Ephraim's meals and exercise routine.

Eventually Ephraim got help and he started eating normally. Through talking over his problems with his therapist, Ephraim discovered that his main problem was linked to his concerns about his father, who had mental health problems of his own. Ephraim was the only boy in his family and, as he was going through his adolescence, he had lost his father figure because of his father's mental health problem. This meant that, for Ephraim, the changes he was experiencing going through the different stages of teenage life were too scary and out of control for him. So instead he tried really hard to develop his own sense of control and security for himself by being strict with his eating and exercising. Unfortunately, Ephraim got caught up in an anorexic way of being and became very unwell.

Talking about this made him free himself to loosen up a bit and eventually try to experience the joys and pains of being a teenager.

NEED HELP?

If you are worried about your eating habits and are confused as to how someone like you can develop an eating disorder, then use some of the contacts in Helpful Organisations (page 95), and talk to someone in confidence about what you are experiencing. That way you will get the advice you need to get the right help for your problem.

CHAPTER SIX:

REDUCING YOUR WEIGHT TO MAKE YOURSELF FEEL GOOD
Some signs of anorexia nervosa

This chapter looks at the physical and emotional signs that someone suffering from anorexia nervosa may have.

Richard Morton first wrote about the illness we now call anorexia nervosa in 1694 in his book *A Nervous Consumption*. From that time until the twentieth century people found it difficult to describe what type of illness it was. In the 1930s and 1940s the illness was studied closely and doctors decided on the physical and emotional signs we now use to diagnose anorexia nervosa.

PHYSICAL SIGNS

Anorexia nervosa can damage your heath to the point that you can potentially die. This is serious stuff – so please read carefully about some of the physical signs of anorexia nervosa.

Low body weight

In anorexia nervosa the body mass index (BMI, see Chapter 3) is less than 17.5. The body weight can be dangerously low and be as low as

50 per cent or more below what it should be. People who develop anorexia nervosa sometimes fail to gain the weight that is expected during their development and in some cases it can affect their height and ability to grow.

Poor blood circulation

The muscles and fat that help keep our bodies warm need enough food to work properly. So, for a person who is anorexic, the body constantly thinks it is winter. To keep our important organs at a safe temperature level, the body stops sending warm blood to those body parts furthest from the heart, particularly the tips of the fingers and toes. As a result it is common for people with anorexia nervosa to have the following:

■ Raynaud's syndrome – the tips of the fingers and toes are constantly cold and red, white or blue in colour, as a result of poor blood flow, and they can easily become damaged
■ Irregular heart beat
■ Low blood pressure
■ Fast heart rate.

Low body temperature

When you have anorexia nervosa, your body uses all your stores of fat just to keep going, but this can be very dangerous because fat helps us keep warm – a layer of fat underneath our skin protects us from the cold. So, to help make up for lack the lack of warmth, someone with anorexia nervosa can start growing an extra layer of body hair. This is called **lanugo hair** and is a fine layer of hair covering the body all over to help create body warmth in the absence of enough body fat and muscle.

Lack of hormones

Remember we spoke about the **hypothalamus** in Chapter 2? Well this part of the brain regulates very important functions in the body along, with a gland called the **thyroid**. They do this by sending out *hormones*, which give signals for your body during puberty. For girls, an important stage in puberty is getting your periods. When this happens you have reached your **menarche**.

FACT BOX

Menarche [men-ark-ee] is the point at which a girl develops and is able to have periods. This is a sign she is able to get pregnant.

When someone has anorexia nervosa the hypothalamus does not get the right signal from the body to send out these hormones and as result the following can take place:

- Puberty does not begin or gets stopped
- Girls stop having periods. Having no periods is called **amenorrhoea**
- Boys do not produce sperm and stop developing physically
- Loss of interest in the opposite sex
- Food passes more slowly through the stomach
- The **metabolism** is low
- Osteoporosis (weak bones).

Starvation

In extreme cases of anorexia nervosa, the body can fail as a result of major organs not getting enough nutrients to do their jobs properly. Starvation begins and the following problems can occur:

- Poor skin condition – dry skin and nails; thinning scalp hair; lanugo hair (see above); calluses (hard skin) forming on the hands
- Poor brain functioning – seizures
- Poor functioning in the stomach and intestine – constipation, diarrhoea.

CASE STUDY

Jemima, from the age of 12, had developed anorexia nervosa. She had a lot of surgery in her mouth so she had to drink mainly liquids while her mouth healed and then she found it very difficult to go back to eating normally again. Having to wear a brace after the operation had thrown her into the spotlight at school and this scared her a great deal. She remembers the start of her anorexia as a way of distracting herself from intensely disturbing feelings. As she got more and more ill, her parents became more protective of her and this made her feel very secure and safe from a world she was very scared of because of her shyness. Jemima's emotional well-being was affected by this major surgery, on top of the fact that she was just a naturally shy and anxious person.

As time went on, Jemima went down to 4½ stone in weight and needed to go into hospital. She was in and out of hospital for all of her teenage and adult years and found it difficult to eat the food she needed to gain weight. Being in hospital was always difficult for her since she would gain the weight only because other people wanted her to. In fact, when she was in hospital, in her own mind she dared nurses and doctors to get her to eat and got into many battles around food. Often when she came out she would lose the weight again. These battles sometimes occurred at home as well.

Jemima did not do these things because she was difficult; she did them because she was frightened and suspicious of all these people who wanted her to put weight on. At times she would see the reason for the need to get to a healthier weight, but then the fear of fat and putting weight on would take over, causing her to resist any encouragement to gain weight.

Jemima's physical ailments were extensive. Because she was so young when it all started, Jemima never got her periods and, as she approached 20 years of age, still looked like a 13 year old. However, because she never had periods, in her late teens she developed osteoporosis. It bothered her a bit that she had the bones of an 80 year old, but still she felt unable to gain weight.

Over time, Jemima has learned to come to terms with her illness and follows a plan created to help her keep her weight in the normal range. She continues to go to hospital once or twice a month to see a doctor to be checked, to review how her plan is going and also to have a chance to talk.

EMOTIONAL SIGNS

If anorexia nervosa were purely a physical condition, then it would be easy for someone suffering from it to do something to put weight on. If you've noticed, every time the illness is mentioned in this book, the whole term **anorexia nervosa** is used. This is because there is a difference between **anorexia** and **anorexia nervosa**. Anorexia on its own refers to a particular weight range (as discussed in Chapter 3), whereas the illness has the word 'nervosa' in it as well as the word 'anorexia'. This is because 'nervosa' refers to the anxiety, fear, sadness, anger, hopelessness, low self-esteem and other troublesome emotions that you experience when you have the condition that make it extremely difficult to gain weight or want to gain weight. Here are some of the emotional signs common in anorexia nervosa.

Valuing thinness

The most widely known fact about anorexia nervosa is that the person suffering from it refuses to gain weight even to the point that they may die. The person is obsessed with their weight and has an almost superhuman determination to become thinner and thinner. They do this by always eating far less than they need to keep their weight the same.

Feeling ineffective

If you suffer from anorexia nervosa, you may be struggling with generally feeling inadequate. Other feelings may be insecurity, worthlessness and also the feeling that you might not be in complete control of your life.

Body dissatisfaction

We looked at body dissatisfaction and body image in Chapter 3. In anorexia nervosa body dissatisfaction is closely linked to the changes that occur as a result of puberty. The shape and size changes that occur in the body are mainly around the hips, legs, breasts (for girls) and penis (for boys) and someone with anorexia nervosa sees these as 'fatness' rather that being a necessary part of development.

Fear of growing up

Sometimes growing up is far more hassle than it's worth. The stages we go through during adolescence (see the table in Chapter 5) can give us some very scary challenges in terms of how we think about ourselves and others as well as how we look or what we do for a living. Because eating helps us grow and develop, an effect of anorexia nervosa is to allow the person suffering from it to stay in or go back to childhood, where they can escape the demand of growing into an adult, which can be quite overwhelming.

Nothing less than perfect

Sometimes people feel that anything they achieve must be the absolute best – no excuses! If you are like this, what you expect of yourself is far more than you can realistically achieve. Hard work does sometimes allow you to achieve those unrealistically high standards for a while. However, as soon as you have to deal with another stress, such as moving house or going to university, it becomes increasingly difficult to keep up that level of hard work. So if you feel you must be perfect all the time, you could be putting yourself under pressure to be perfect at all costs – even if this affects your health, and might lead to anorexia nervosa.

Difficulty in forming relationships

Sometimes people feel unable to express emotions in a comfortable way towards others. Low self-esteem and low self-worth often make you feel that you are so out-of-the-ordinary or such a 'geek' that others do not truly want to be your friend. It can be so bad, that if people do genuinely want to be your friend you don't believe them and you become suspicious about their intentions and so may even stop the relationship before it develops. Perhaps this shyness is how you always were and as you became a teenager and the pressure to form new friends grew, so your anxiety about the whole thing grew.

Lack of awareness of inner feelings

This is probably the most common emotional problem in people suffering from anorexia nervosa. It is about your lack of confidence in recognising your emotions in response to things and, also, your ability to accurately identify the feelings of hunger for and satisfaction by food. People with anorexia nervosa often mistake 'hunger' for 'greed'. If they experience difficult feelings such as guilt, anger and sadness, they may mistake them as being full or just simply call them 'fat'.

For me it's a disease of the mind. Some days, it still happens to me. What happens is that I feel fear about something, but rather than registering I feel fear about it, I go 'I feel fat' and relay how I feel to my body and the way that I look at myself – it's completely distorted. It's taken time to really let go of that.

Geri Halliwell, pop star

NEED HELP?

Seeking help is often difficult. Often the first step is realising there is a problem; this can be the most difficult step to take. In Helpful Organisations on page 95, you will find useful tips and a list of contacts.

The next two chapters look at bulimia nervosa.

CHAPTER SEVEN:

A QUESTIONNAIRE ON BULIMIA NERVOSA
Symptoms to look out for

If you think that you or someone close to you has bulimia nervosa, complete this questionnaire. Your responses will show if you have any problems.

BULIMIA NERVOSA QUESTIONNAIRE

Read each question carefully then choose the answer that fits closest with your experience.

1 Do you eat regularly every day?
- **a** I'm pretty sure I do
- **b** I try my best to
- **c** I skip meals sometimes during the day

2 Do you go on strict diets?
- **a** No need
- **b** I try to eat healthily, but I do believe in treating myself
- **c** Most definitely

---

3 Does breaking your diet once mean you are a complete failure?

a Diets are for wimps anyway

b Diets are a slippery slope and do more harm than good

c Yes, absolutely

4 Even when you are not on a diet, do you make sure to keep your calories down?

a I have absolutely no idea about calories

b I am aware of the calories in things but I don't let that affect me

c I have to with my size

5 Have you ever fasted the whole day?

a I have tried once or twice

b No, this would only make me feel too hungry the next day

c Yes, three or more times a week

6 Do you take diet pills to help you lose weight?

a Life's too short

b No

c Yes, once to five times a day

7 Do you take diuretics to help you lose weight?

a I tried it once, but never again

b No

c Yes, once to five times a day

8 Do you take laxatives to help you lose weight?

a Just to ease discomfort

b Only for constipation

c Yes, once to five times a day

9 Do you make yourself vomit to help you lose weight?
a I like my food too much
b No
c Yes, three times a week to daily

10 Does your pattern of eating severely interfere with your life?
a I try not to let it
b Eating is part of life
c Constantly, if I could do without eating I would

11 Does food dominate your life?
a I won't let it
b No
c Constantly

12 Do you eat and eat until physical discomfort is what stops you?
a Is that possible?
b When I feel satisfied I stop eating
c Yes, at times

13 Is food all you think about sometimes?
a I can't really tell you
b No, there more important things to think about
c Yes, it feels like I am constantly thinking about food

14 Do you always eat much more when you're on your own than you do in front of others?
a It doesn't matter where or what I eat
b I tend to eat according to what I need and how hungry I am
c Definitely, people would be horrified otherwise

15 Can it be a problem for you to stop eating when you want to?

a I don't understand

b I don't think so

c Yes

16 Is the overpowering urge to eat and eat a problem for you?

a I don't really see it as a problem

b No

c Yes, it is agonising

17 Do you tend to eat loads when you get anxious?

a I don't really get anxious

b Not really, I try to talk it over with someone

c All the time

18 How does the thought of becoming fat make you feel?

a How fat?

b Not too bothered

c Absolutely terrified

19 How often do you eat large amounts of food, not necessarily meals, rapidly?

a Only when I'm really enjoying it

b Never

c From two to three times a week to once or more times a day

20 How ashamed are you of your eating habits?

a Never really thought of it

b Not at all

c I feel very ashamed

When you have finished add up how many *a*s, *b*s and *c*s you circled and read what your answers may indicate.

WHAT YOUR ANSWERS MEAN

Mostly *a*s: You definitely enjoy food and have not given it much thought at all in terms of how it is connected to your emotions. This can be a healthy way to be but it might be that you are not entirely sure about how much food and eating are truly affecting you.

Mostly *b*s: This shows quite a balanced, healthy approach to food and eating. Food and eating are functional to your life, you do not use them as a way of helping with emotional issues and you are in control.

Mostly *c*s: You are more than likely suffering from a poor body image and have difficult attitudes to eating. Please have a look at Chapters 11–14 to get professional help.

Mostly a mixture of *a*s and *b*s: A very healthy position, you enjoy your food and have little problems as a result. More than likely you are reading this book because you are worried about someone else.

Mostly a mixture of *a*s and *c*s: These are extreme but opposite responses, which may mean that you are confused about what you are experiencing. You might benefit from having a chat with someone about your situation. Look at Helpful Organisations for useful people to contact.

CHAPTER EIGHT:

DOES MY BUM LOOK BIG IN THIS?
The torments of bulimia nervosa

Bulimia nervosa was first properly described in 1979, by Professor Gerald Russell, and given its name by Dr Patrick Campbell, both doctors in the Royal Free Hospital in London.

Bulimia nervosa tends to start when people are between the ages of 16 and 20 years, much older than with anorexia nervosa. Sufferers are often struggling with this illness as well as doing their GCSEs or A-levels or even a job. Often, someone with bulimia nervosa either will have had or will go on to get anorexia nervosa.

Although bulimia nervosa is a very serious illness, people with it tend to wait a very long time to seek help, and sometimes they never do. In fact some people with bulimia nervosa can even see it as helpful in dealing with their eating habits, but this is a dangerous view. It is often very difficult to recover from this illness and it can have lasting bad effects on health.

This chapter looks at the physical and emotional signs that someone suffering from bulimia nervosa may have.

PHYSICAL SIGNS

Bingeing

Bingeing – uncontrollable overeating – is the main problem for someone who is **bulimic**. So a bulimic binge will involve both:

1 Eating too much at one go – eating an amount of food during an amount of time (e.g. within two hours) that is definitely much more than most people would eat during the same time and under the same circumstances, and

2 A feeling of lack of control over what you are eating during that time, particularly the feeling that you cannot control what or how much you are eating.

Purging

The other main problem of bulimia nervosa is purging – getting rid of the food you've eaten – or the **compensatory behaviours** we saw in Chapter 1.

Some examples of purging actions are:

- Making yourself vomit
- Exercising far more than is necessary
- Using laxatives and enemas when there is no need to
- Using **diuretics**: this medication gets rid of water from your body; it makes you pass a lot of urine so you can lose a lot of weight as a result
- Fasting for no religious or medical reason
- Taking other medication that causes weight loss, when you don't need to be taking it.

The bingeing and purging cycle

If someone binges and then purges themselves over and over again, they may do this at least twice a week and as much as several times every day. If they keep on bingeing and purging in this way for about three months or more, then they are suffering from an eating disorder.

Signs of vomiting

Vomiting is a common way of making up for the binges and causes a number of difficulties.

1 Dental problems – the stomach acid that comes up with the food that is brought back up can wear away your teeth enamel.

2 Reduction of important chemicals in the body – excess vomiting can remove vital chemicals from your body, and this can be very dangerous. Potassium in the body helps our heart beat regularly so removing too much of it can cause serious health problems; having too little potassium in the body called **hypokalaemia**.

3 Calluses (hard skin) on knuckles – from the wear and tear caused by using your fingers to help bring about vomiting. These are called Russell marks.

4 Sore throat – caused by the acid in the stomach coming up during vomiting.

5 An uncontrollable urge to leave the table after meals – your body starts absorbing calories and nutrients very soon after you eat so someone with bulimia nervosa often tries to get rid of food right after they've eaten it. It also gets more difficult to bring food back up the longer you leave it in your stomach.

Frequent weight changes

Because someone with bulimia nervosa makes up for their bingeing by somehow getting rid of the food immediately, their weight may go up and down but tends to stay mainly within and around the normal BMI. Depending on whether you binge more than you make up for it

or purge yourself more than you binge, then you may be overweight
or underweight.

Tiredness

Taking the body through the cycle of bingeing and then doing things
to get rid of all that food can be quite tiring so people who do this end
up feeling very drained.

Swollen salivary (parotid) glands

Bingeing and vomiting make your salivary glands work very hard to
produce enough saliva to help the food slip down easily and then up
again. This saliva is needed to help protect your mouth from your
stomach acid. As a result the salivary glands become swollen,
sometimes to the size of table tennis balls.

Irregular periods

Your weight affects your hormones and your hormones regulate your
menstruation (your periods). So if your weight goes up and down as
a result of bulimia nervosa, your periods can become irregular. This
weight and hormone fluctuation can even lead to your ovaries being
affected, and **cysts** or little balls may form on your ovaries. This is
called **Poly Cystic Ovarian Syndrome** (PCOS) and can result in long
lasting difficulties with your hormones and your ability to have children.

Poor skin condition

People wanting to be thin often avoid eating fatty food or they
immediately get rid of it after eating it. However, avoiding all fatty food
can result in your skin and hair becoming dry and in poor condition.

EMOTIONAL SIGNS

The 'bulimia' in bulimia nervosa means having the appetite of a bull and this refers to the bingeing that people do. The 'nervosa' means the emotional and psychological states people experience during the illness (in a similar way to how we mentioned it in anorexia nervosa in Chapter 6).

Valuing thinness and having uncontrollable hunger

Someone with bulimia nervosa has a desperate fear of fatness and constantly tries to lose weight through many ways. However, they often suddenly stop their efforts to lose weight because they are experiencing very difficult emotions. Although these emotions can be caused by all sorts of things, they make someone with bulimia nervosa feel hungry and the person then doesn't deal with the causes of their emotions.

How I look affects how I feel about me

If you have bulimia nervosa, you think that the way you look is what matters and your feelings depend on how you look. Remember our discussion earlier on *Identity* in Chapter 5? Well, sometimes when you are insecure about *who* you are, you feel everyone is judging you by *what* you look like on the outside. This can make you focus on your appearance, weight and shape, and perhaps even try to adjust them. People who feel insecure about how they look are sometimes desperate to look like what is accepted in society and can be very influenced by the media. Being uncomfortable with how you look can make you follow fashion, even if it doesn't always suit you as a person.

Food is an obsession

If you get rid of food by vomiting, laxative abuse, over-exercising and other forms of purging, you are also getting rid of vital nutrients and calories, so your body thinks it is being starved. So, the part of your brain that drives you to look for food starts up, making you constantly think of food because it thinks you need some help in remembering what it is in order to find it. As a result, you are always thinking and talking of food and become obsessed with the sight and smell of food. You might start keeping a lot of food magazines and watching cooking programmes.

The more you starve yourself of food, the more your brain makes you think of food. And because you wanted to avoid food in the first place, this makes you feel even worse. Your body, however, recognises that you need to eat to survive in spite of your efforts to deny yourself nourishment.

Distorted view of weight and shape

Sometimes the effort to reduce weight or change your shape is so strong that you begin to lose sight of what you really look like to the point that your mind plays tricks on you.

CASE STUDY

I hate catching my reflection in the shop windows and mirrors as I walk along because I look so fat and out of shape. I get a shudder whenever I see my reflection and have to prepare myself because I know I would see this huge monster staring back at me.

One day I was walking along Oxford Street, when in front of this shoe store I was drawn to these gorgeous sandals in the shop window. I caught sight of this girl staring back at me. 'She must have been standing to the side of me a little way behind', I thought, so I turned to see who was looking right into my eyes. When I turned around, I realised it was me – no one else was around – and due to the funny angle of the mirror, it appeared to be someone else. When I turned back to look at the reflection, I swear the reflection had grown in size, particularly around my waist, thighs and face! In total I went up in size by about two dress sizes. I became repulsed by my own reflection.

This really freaked me out because as soon as I realised that it was me, the reflection no longer looked normal! That was when I realised I had a problem and needed help. I thought the judgement I had of myself was accurate but something felt wrong. **M,19**

Many people with bulimia nervosa are successful and hold quite high positions of responsibility. However, the pressures that come with such a position can be enormous and can cause feelings of low self-esteem when they become too much. Perhaps these high-powered positions demand that people show a level of self-confidence that inside they don't really feel they have. Being the captain of a swimming team or a store manager can be quite demanding, so you might turn to bingeing and getting rid of food to cope with the pressures that come with the job.

Your emotional well-being gets affected

Any eating disorder can cause some problems with your emotional well-being:

- Anxiety: you can become so anxious that you may get panic attacks where you really think that you are going to die and you begin to gasp for breath and feel very afraid.
- Depression: bingeing and vomiting regularly can make you feel extremely sad about your situation as being bulimic is not a proper solution – nothing changes for the better, not even your body.

When you feel sad to the point that you do not feel able to clean yourself or your surroundings, get enjoyment from anything or do the simplest of things, then you are depressed.

Low self-esteem

You place a very low value on yourself, which gets even lower when you become more desperate in your efforts to lose weight. If you become dependent on food and feel out of control but you present a normal, happy image of yourself to people, you might start feeling like a fake on top of everything else.

Shame and guilt

Someone with bulimia nervosa can use eating and bingeing to feel better about stressful situations. However, guilt, embarrassment and secrecy are difficult feelings that often follow a binge and this can make you feel even worse about yourself.

Emotional behaviour and mood swings

Being afraid to take a closer look at how you feel can cause you to become confused about your emotions. But then it may feel quite frightening to keep your emotions inside and they come out in ways you find difficult to control.

Impulsive behaviour

As you get more out of control, you can begin to act more and more on impulse without taking time to think of the consequences. Some impulsive things that people suffering from bulimia nervosa might do include:

■ Drug abuse (to lose weight or feel happy)
■ Alcohol abuse (to feel relaxed)

- Stealing (mainly food for bingeing or cosmetics)
- Sexual behaviour with several people (to feel wanted or loved)
- Self-harm (often cutting or burning yourself).

I feel helpless and lonely

Bulimia nervosa is an illness of secrecy and guilt so you might have to do things that other people would find difficult to understand. You will feel helpless against the urge to binge and get rid of your food and this in turn may mean you make your bulimia more important than being close to your friends and family. This can lead to you being quite isolated and feeling very lonely.

Conflict and deceit in your relationships with people

As your bulimia becomes more and more important in your life and more out of control, you may become desperate enough to deceive those closest to you. Stealing food from flatmates or the cupboards in your family home is something that is hard to resist when you need to binge and you have run out of food and money. However, this can make other people angry and you might then deny taking anything. If you are not ready to face up to your problem, your relationships can suffer as a result.

Difficult experiences in childhood

People can use bingeing and vomiting to block out difficult memories from childhood. Physical or sexual abuse that happened to you or that you witnessed can be something that you do not want to remember and makes you feel bad about yourself. Bulimia can provide a temporary solution, but it definitely makes the situation worse in the end.

NEED HELP?

Seeking help can be difficult. Often the first step, which can be the most difficult, is realising there is a problem. The most effective way of getting out of bulimia nervosa is recognising how you think and the link this has with your emotions. In Helpful Organisations you will find information on the help available as well as a list of useful contacts.

The next chapter looks at binge eating disorder.

CHAPTER NINE:

HOW SUCCESSFUL IS FOOD IN EASING YOUR EMOTIONAL PAIN?
Some information about comfort eating and bingeing

Binge eating disorder is similar to bulimia nervosa because the sufferer has bingeing periods, but the sufferer doesn't purge themselves after the bingeing. So, people with this disorder have their weight either:

- just above the normal range, or
- in or above the obese range.

It is important to remember that although binge eating disorder is commonly found in obese people, it is not the same as 'obesity'. So, not all obese people are suffering from a binge eating disorder.

FACT BOX

Binge eating disorder = obese weight range
An obese person ≠ binge eating disorder

This chapter looks at the physical and emotional signs that someone suffering from binge eating disorder may have.

PHYSICAL SIGNS

High body weight

Someone who develops a binge eating disorder usually has a large build or may have always found it difficult to lose weight. This could be because they have inherited this from their family (it is genetic) or because in their family or culture, it was common to eat larger meals than in the rest of the society around them. So, before they developed a binge eating disorder their weight may have been at the upper end of normal. If they had positive images of food and eating when they were growing up in their family, then they may find it hard to restrict their food intake, and instead they may turn to **comfort eating** when distressed.

Bingeing

Someone with binge eating disorder, will binge (overeat uncontrollably) in a similar way to those people with bulimia nervosa by:

- Eating much more rapidly than normal
- Eating until they feel uncomfortably full
- Eating large amounts of food when they are not physically hungry
- Eating alone because of embarrassment over how much they are eating
- Feeling disgusted with themselves, depressed or very guilty after overeating
- Feeling distress about binge eating
- Binge eating on average at least two days a week for six months.

Illnesses caused by binge eating disorder

The most common physical illnesses caused by binge eating disorder are those that also occur with obesity. These include:

- Diabetes
- High blood pressure
- High cholesterol levels
- Gallbladder disease
- Heart disease
- Some forms of cancer.

EMOTIONAL SIGNS

Not wanting to be thin

I know I should lose the weight, but I am terrified to lose it because I am afraid of what would be left. I like the type of person I am but I know my size is very unhealthy. Deep down I am afraid I would also stop being me if I become thin.

Melanie, 34

Someone suffering from binge eating disorder does not get rid of the food by purging, so after the binge, they don't do anything else. Sometimes, they could be bingeing day after day. They would still always be thinking about weight loss and really want to lose weight, but they don't want to be thin so their effort to lose weight is not that strong.

Food is used to make difficult emotions go away

Someone with a binge eating disorder often finds it difficult to deal with negative emotions. Examples of such feelings are:

- Guilt
- Sadness
- Shame
- Anger.

Not being able to deal with negative emotions is a problem because we all at some time or another will experience them. Food and eating can provide comfort by distracting you from these emotions. Getting caught up in the act of eating during a binge is enough to move your thoughts away from what is upsetting you.

EATING DISORDERS NOT OTHERWISE SPECIFIED (EDNOS)
Other less well known eating disorders and food related illnesses

EDNOS

In Chapters 6 to 9, we looked the three main eating disorders in some detail. As we said in Chapter 2, there is another eating disorder diagnosis called **eating disorders not otherwise specified (EDNOS)**, which refers to an eating disorder that is made up of features of two or more of the three main eating disorders – anorexia nervosa, bulimia nervosa and binge eating disorder.

The most common eating disorder is actually EDNOS, and it is also the eating disorder most on the increase and can be difficult to recover from. So, if you have a mixture of the signs from all the three major eating disorders, then it would be hard to say for certain which of the eating disorders you suffer from, and this might be quite distressing for you. It can also be confusing for the health professional who is helping you because some things that may be helpful for one disorder may not be so helpful for another.

For example, to help someone with anorexia nervosa, you must help them find a way to put weight on; to help someone with bulimia nervosa, you would try to get them to accept the way they are now; to help someone with binge eating disorder, you would need to help them to find a way to reduce their weight and eat less. But if you have EDNOS, you have a mixture of problems from two or all three of the other disorders at any one time. The good news is that there are ways to help you if you suffer from EDNOS – so don't despair!

OTHER THAN EDNOS

There are some other less well known eating disorders and problems associated with eating. If you as a young person feel increasing pressure from society that you should look a certain way, then the ways in which others view you and your body can become more and more important to you.

Eating in a certain way can help you change your body. However, as eating is so much a part of our lives, it is quite easy for the way we eat and the reasons we eat to be affected by things other than our body image. It is very easy to suffer not only from eating disorders, but also from **disordered eating**. Disordered eating means having eating patterns that are not normal and some people suffer from them because of:

- psychological difficulties
- learning difficulties
- genetic disorders
- physical problems.

The rest of this chapter lists some other food-related illnesses and examples of disordered eating.

Anorexia athletica (compulsive exercising)

This is not an illness in its own right. The behaviours that **anorexia athletica** describes are usually a part of anorexia nervosa, bulimia nervosa or an **obsessive-compulsive disorder** (see Chapter 4).

If you suffer from this problem, you
- repeatedly exercise beyond the need for good fitness
- may be a fanatic about weight and diet
- would rather exercise than go to school, go to work or be with friends or family
- always challenge yourself
- forget that physical activity can be fun
- define your self-worth in terms of your performance
- are rarely or never satisfied with your athletic achievements
- do not take time to celebrate when you win
- push on to the next challenge immediately
- justify your excessive behaviour by saying you are a 'special' athlete.

FACT BOX

Obsessive-compulsive disorder: *An illness where the person feels that they must do certain things in a certain way for fear of something terrible happening.*

Many people who are preoccupied with food and weight exercise compulsively to try to control their weight. It is important to remember here that the real issues are not weight and good performance but are rather control and self-respect.

Anorexia nervosa in young children

Sometimes the signs typical of anorexia nervosa appear suddenly in a young child. Also, children with this anorexic-type condition can suddenly get worse very quickly, for no obvious reason.

The cause of this condition is not known but it may be related to infections from some serious childhood diseases. A child could have recently had a chest, throat or other infection just before developing the so-called 'anorexia nervosa'.

Doctors describe this condition as an 'infection-triggered, auto-immune subtype of anorexia nervosa' in young children. Auto-immune refers to the situation when the defences of the body that are designed to attack and destroy foreign bodies that cause infection, turn on the body itself and start attacking it. The first step in treatment is to see a specialist doctor.

Bigorexia

This is also known as **muscle dysmorphia** or **reverse anorexia**. It is a relatively new disorder and occurs mainly in men and boys and in people who body build. If you have this problem you exercise obsessively because you falsely believe your body is too small or not muscular enough. No matter how much you work out you still feel puny, leading you to hide from other people or wear baggy clothing to disguise your body shape.

Body dysmorphic disorder

'Dysmorphia' can be defined as a distorted judgement of beauty. A person with an eating disorder says, 'I am so fat', whereas a person with body dysmorphic disorder (or BDD) says, 'I am so ugly'.

BDD is thought to be a kind of **obsessive-compulsive disorder** rather than a type of anorexia nervosa or bulimia nervosa and often includes social **phobias** (an irrational and uncontrollable fear of something). BDD affects people usually before they are about 18 years old. People suffering with BDD are shy and withdrawn in new situations and with unfamiliar people.

If you suffer from BDD, you are excessively concerned about your appearance, and are especially convinced that something is wrong with your face, hair and skin. Your friends and family can see nothing wrong with you and try to reassure you but, as a BDD sufferer, you do not believe them. Having plastic surgery is something that you often think about.

BDD is treatable with either medication or psychotherapy (see Chapter 13).

FACT BOX

Psychotherapy: *Treatment involving talking about your situation in a way that helps you to change your thoughts and emotions through a greater understanding of them.*

Chewing and spitting

Someone with this condition would put food into their mouth, taste it, chew it and then spit it out. This is not an eating disorder on its own, but a way of controlling the amount of calories eaten, and is often used by those with anorexia nervosa, and sometimes bulimia nervosa and EDNOS.

Chewing and spitting allows someone to experience some enjoyment of food but to avoid the intake of calories. But, as the person is not actually eating the essential nutrients, chewing and spitting can be just as harmful to their health as starvation dieting and binge eating followed by purging.

Cyclic vomiting syndrome

This condition is characterised by cycles of frequent vomiting, and is most usually found in children. It may be related to migraine headaches.

Gourmand syndrome

Someone with this syndrome is preoccupied with fine food, including buying, preparing, presenting and eating it. It is very rare and thought to be caused by injury to the brain.

Night-eating syndrome

If you suffered from night-eating syndrome you would:
- have little or no appetite for breakfast
- delay your first meal for several hours after waking up
- often be upset about how much you ate the night before
- eat most of your food late in the day or at night.

Nocturnal sleep-related eating disorder

This is thought to be a sleep disorder, not an eating disorder, where you would sleep-eat and you may sleep-walk as well.

Orthorexia nervosa

This is not an illness in its own right. **Orthorexia nervosa** describes an abnormally strong interest in eating 'proper' or 'pure' or 'superior' food. People with orthorexia nervosa feel superior to others who eat 'improper' food, which might include non-organic or 'junk' foods and food found in regular grocery stores, as opposed to healthfood stores. Orthorexics worry constantly over:

- What to eat
- How much to eat
- How to prepare food 'properly'
- Where to obtain 'pure' and 'proper' foods.

Eating the 'right' food becomes an important, or even the most important thing in life. If you suffer from this problem, then you view how good you are in terms of what you do or do not eat. Your personal values, relationships and career goals become less important than the quality and timing of what you eat. This problem might be a type of **obsessive-compulsive disorder**.

Pica

This is a craving to eat non-food items such as dirt, clay, plaster, chalk or paint chips.

Prader–Willi syndrome

This is a problem that is present from birth and is commonly associated with learning difficulties and behavioural problems.

Someone with it feels the need to eat constantly but their brain is unable to tell them they are full up.

Rumination syndrome

Someone with this syndrome eats, swallows and then brings up food from their stomach back into their mouth, where they chew it and swallow it again. This may be repeated several times or for several hours per episode. The person may be doing this deliberately or they may not be able to help it. Someone with this syndrome may say that their vomited food does not taste bitter, and they may be able to return it to their mouth gently, rather than by loud vomiting.

Yo-yo dieting

This is when you constantly go on new diets. You try a new diet, but then stop the diet because it only worked for a short time or was too difficult to stick to, so your weight goes up, so you try another new diet, and so on, resulting in your weight going up and down. This can lead you to become so distressed about yourself that you can develop an eating disorder if you always try to make yourself feel better by adjusting your weight.

WHAT NEXT?

Chapters 11 to 13 will look at the different types of help available to you, and Helpful Organisations lists some useful organisations that can offer you help.

CHAPTER ELEVEN:

STARTING TO GET OVER EATING DISORDERS
The road to recovery

GETTING BETTER IS NOT AS EASY AS IT LOOKS TO OTHERS

Some people think that it is easy for someone to stop being anorexic and to start eating properly or for someone to get over bulimia by eating regular meals or for someone who suffers from binge eating disorder to just go on a diet. So people can get very angry with those who suffer with eating disorders. But it is not as simple as it sounds. Moving from being a sufferer to a survivor of an eating disorder takes a lot of help from health professionals as well as family members over a long period of time.

MOTIVATION

W R Miller, a psychologist, did a lot of research into human motivation and the part it played in helping people give up harmful habits. He focused on people who had drink problems. His findings have been used in boosting the motivation of people with eating disorders to change their eating habits, and it has been proven to be a very effective way of working. He had this to say about motivation.

Motivation can be understood not as something that one has but something one does. It involves recognising a problem, searching for a way to change, and then beginning and sticking with that change strategy.

W R Miller, 1995

In order for you to change, there must be enough reasons for you to *want* to change or enough reasons for you at least to not want to stay where you are. Eating disorders can develop at a time when things in your life are stressing you out so much that you may not even realise that what you are doing is harmful. Your situation may get to a point that you can get very ill as a result of your eating disorder, putting your life at risk and still not think that anything is wrong. Then you might think that anyone trying to help you is interfering or wanting to control you, so you might not want to talk to them and this can have serious consequences for you.

So, if you need help or someone you know needs help, you have to think carefully about how to get help to change.

HOW DO I BEGIN TO CHANGE? THE DIFFERENT STAGES:

1 **Don't even go there!** The first step to changing a problem is to think that it *is* a problem. If you see nothing wrong with what you are doing, then why change? So, this stage is to ask yourself whether your eating is a problem or not.

2 **Thinking about it:** The next stage is when your behaviour is beginning to stop you from getting on with your life so much that you worry about it more and more. You start testing out how bad your situation is and whether you are making a mountain out of a molehill by confiding in others about your situation. Usually people either try to offer help themselves or support you as you think about seeking professional help. Reading this book means that you are probably in the 'Thinking about it' phase, if you are concerned for yourself.

3 **Seeking help:** This is when you decide you want to get over your problems and get healthy.

4 **Get into action:** This is when you are receiving treatment for your eating disorder and hopefully making changes, although at times this may seem to be the most difficult thing you have ever done!

5 **Keeping it up:** The underlying issues that led you to have an eating disorder have been with you for a long time and so, after getting rid of an eating disorder, you have to keep working really hard to make sure that these issues do not return.

6 **Temporary lapse:** One thing you will have learned during your recovery is not to be too hard on yourself. At some point after getting rid of your eating disorder, you might suffer a moment of weakness resulting in a relapse, but this is a necessary part of change because it highlights the things you might have missed first time. A relapse might make you even stronger.

CHAPTER TWELVE:

CASE STUDY
I can switch it on or off!

Tanya, a 16-year-old girl of African Caribbean origin, disclosed to a school counsellor that she sometimes binged and then vomited. When the counsellor asked her why she did this, she replied that she was fed up of not being able to wear the same clothes as her friends in school because they did not suit her shape. She felt that her bum was too big and, although having a large bum was common in women from her background, it was not that common for other girls in her school, who were mainly white, so it annoyed her.

So, Tanya would vomit after meals in order to lose weight whenever she felt she needed to and would then stop when she had reached the size she wanted. 'It isn't related to stress or anything like that. I am in control of this and I don't need any help. Looking like my peers is very important and this is a quick and easy way for me to achieve that. To be honest, I don't think this will ever be a problem because I can switch it on or off as I like.'

Tanya was convinced that she had her bulimia under control and did not want any help. In fact, the problems she had fitting in because of her body shape were more troubling to her than any difficulties caused by her bulimia. You could say she didn't have any **motivation to change**.

After reading Chapter 9, you will know that there are many health and emotional problems experienced by someone who is bulimic. Tanya, however, did not see her bulimia nervosa as a problem.

So, why did she tell the counsellor? Perhaps she knew inside that bulimia was risky to her health, but she still wanted to believe that it was not a problem for her. Her body shape was of more concern to her than how dangerous the bulimia was. The fact that Tanya told someone else about her bulimia could mean that, on some level, she was worried about what she was doing, but she was not at the stage of thinking of it as a problem.

What do you think would be the best way to help Tanya to *want* to do something about her bulimia?

Here are some possible solutions:

1 You could ask Tanya to explain to you how important it was for her to fit in and when you got where she was coming from, tell her that you understand her. It would be important for Tanya to believe that you do understand her or *empathise* with her, because remember, bulimia is about what you do on the outside to make how you feel on the inside a bit better.

2 Tanya is using a very harmful method of fitting in. Try to offer her information about what harm she is doing to herself through her bulimia.

3 Most importantly, advise her to seek professional help when she feels even slightly out of control. An eating disorder can start in what appears to be a harmless way, but it slowly takes over and seriously affects your emotional and physical health.

You could also talk to someone who is qualified to help about the advice you are offering Tanya and what emotions that is stirring up in you. Remember always to look after yourself, as well as your friends!

CHAPTER THIRTEEN:

SOME HELPFUL REMEDIES
Learning to eat healthily again

GETTING HELP TO EAT PROPERLY AGAIN

For some people with an eating disorder, getting help from a hospital might be the only way for them to get back their health. The government's Department of Health has published guidelines on what help you should expect from health professionals.

The main guidelines are:

- You should be able to get most of your treatment without having to stay overnight in the hospital.
- If your eating disorder is so bad that your life is at risk, you then should go into hospital for a few days and nights. There, specially trained staff will support you and your treatment to bring your weight back up to the normal body mass index.
- Your relatives and friends should also get support to help them cope with someone they love having an eating disorder.
- If you are still unable to make yourself eat and your life is still at risk, you can be fed against your will in order to keep you alive. The

law and/or the consent of your parents or guardians can be used against your will to give you the necessary treatment.

CHALLENGING THOUGHTS AND BEHAVIOURS

We have looked at the link between our mind and body as well as the link between eating and emotions. So one of the most successful ways of getting over an eating disorder is to focus on your:

■ Thoughts
■ Emotions
■ Behaviours.

It is important for you to be able to identify the emotions that are stirred up by certain words or situations in your life. Also, identifying the actions you then take to help you deal with those negative emotions can be useful. When you do this, you can understand why your thoughts about certain situations can make you feel horrible, so then you start to find ways to change your emotions about these situations.

For example, it can be helpful to write down your thoughts and then the emotions you experience around eating (whether it is a normal meal or a binge) and/or an episode of purging (on the toilet after taking laxatives, in the toilet vomiting, exercising or when doing whatever you do to lose calories). Using the list below as a guide of what to write about, you may get an indication of what the underlying problems are for you.

■ Date and time of day
■ Amount and type of food
■ What time and how did I get rid of it?

- What were the thoughts in my head at the time?
- What emotions was I feeling before and after?

TALKING ABOUT YOUR FEELINGS

A lot of the issues around eating disorders are about how you feel about yourself and what you think about yourself. So, talking about these is a major part of the treatment of eating disorders. Treatment involving talking about your situation in a way that helps you to change your thoughts and emotions through a greater understanding of them is called **psychotherapy**.

Psychotherapy can be done either in groups (group psychotherapy) or by you on your own talking to one person (individual psychotherapy). Psychotherapy can focus on:

- Helping you to find the meaning of your inner feelings and of things that have happened in your past (psychoanalytic psychotherapy)
- Your relationships with other people (interpersonal psychotherapy)
- Finding out how you think and how your thoughts affect your behaviour (cognitive behavioural therapy)
- How your relationships with other people are affected by what you do, which in turn affects you in a circular way (systemic psychotherapy)
- Stopping you acting on impulse to deal with your difficult emotions which can help you to identify and better understand them (dialectical behavioural therapy).

GET HEALTHY ADVICE ABOUT FOOD AND NUTRITION

One of the basic problems to deal with in an eating disorder is getting back the nutrients you are losing out on. A balanced, healthy diet will prevent the physical problems of eating disorders, which can sometimes lead to severe malnutrition, obesity and even death.

LEARNING TO EAT AGAIN

This is the part of getting better from an eating disorder that appears to be the easiest, but in fact can be the most difficult. People who suffer from eating disorders can often have a very good knowledge of what and how to eat. The problem is that they have such low self-worth that they don't think food will affect them in the same way as other people, so they can become frightened of eating normally.

For example, if you have binge eating disorder, you might be eating out of despair from thinking that you can never lose weight anyway so why bother. If you have bulimia nervosa, then you might find it difficult to get out of the bingeing and vomiting cycle, so you dare not stop doing it for fear of gaining weight. If you suffer from anorexia nervosa, then your fear of fat and weight gain might make you think that you are unable to eat a normal meal. You might even believe that normal eating doesn't apply to you.

So all eating disorder sufferers should aim to eat normally. Here are some tips on how to get back on track with eating if you are struggling with eating normally.

■ Breakfast is the MOST important meal of the day, so every day make sure to eat your breakfast – DO NOT SKIP BREAKFAST!

Breakfast is the first meal that *breaks* an 8 –12-hour *fast*, which occurs when you are asleep. The body works extremely hard whilst you are asleep to replenish itself and this uses a lot of energy. And believe me, you need a good source of food and nutrients when you wake up to start a new day. Missing out breakfast deprives you of a much needed nutrition refill. Going without it would leave you run down, lower your metabolism and leave you feeling not fully satisfied during the day.

■ Find out what serving size is right for you. Your doctor's surgery will have very helpful leaflets on healthy eating.

■ DO NOT DIET!!

■ Try to have a healthy balance of all food groups – fats, carbohydrates and proteins. Remember that if you leave out any food groups from what you eat, the body makes up for this by reducing your metabolic rate and this leaves you feeling low in energy.

SEEK PROFESSIONAL HELP

This book is not a substitute for help, it is simply about equipping you with the information you need to decide whether you need to be concerned, how much to be concerned and where to go to get help.

Reading this book can be a sign that you are in the 'Thinking about it' stage (see Chapter 11), so you are curious about what you or someone close to you may be experiencing.

Visiting your doctor

If you feel you need help from a professional, then your family doctor (or GP, general practitioner) is a very useful person to talk to. This may seem to be a huge step, but your doctor can arrange specialist treatment if you need it, so he or she is a very important person to share your problem with.

If you don't want other people in your family to know, then if you are 16 years or older, you can talk to your doctor in confidence and have the right to ask that what you discuss is kept confidential. This means that your doctor will not talk freely about what you have discussed. But, at the same time, you and your doctor can agree on who can and needs to be told about the discussion. It is very different from a secret.

However, it might be that your problem is at the stage where discussing things in confidence could be dangerous for you, because you might need to go into hospital (see the Department of Health guidelines above).

Visiting your doctor can be scary at first. Also, it is very important that you give your doctor the right information about your problems. So, if you are concerned you might have an eating disorder, here are some things that might be useful to know yourself and to tell your doctor:

1. The type of eating problems you are having – are you not eating enough, are you eating then vomiting or are you eating too much?
2. How long have you been having these eating problems?
3. How do you feel about yourself?
4. Your sleeping pattern – how long do you sleep for and when?
5. How much do you weigh?
6. How much weight have you lost?
7. How much weight have you put on?
8. Have you any aches and pains in your stomach, head, back or limbs?
9. What things worry you about your life?

10 How is your school work being affected – can you concentrate?

Write down your answers to these questions and tell them to your doctor. You may find that this can help you and your doctor discuss quite a lot and so allow your doctor to find the correct help for your problem.

DO NOT SUFFER IN SILENCE

Well, if you have made it this far, you may now have more questions about eating disorders than before you read the book, and that is a good thing.

An eating disorder is a problem that is very difficult to get over, because you have to keep eating while getting over it. That is why it is important to not do it on your own. An eating disorder can affect your view of reality and so trying to get over it completely on your own can sometimes lead you into more problems.

Having said that, sometimes having an eating disorder in the first place is about *wanting* to do things *on your own* and so you will still want to have some independence while you are getting over it. So, some *self-help* books have been written to help people suffering from eating disorders to help themselves. I recommend that, even if you are using a self-help book, you find someone you can meet up with regularly to see if you are on the right track. You never know, a very close friend or family member could have experience with an eating disorder and be a great support to you. This method of getting better is highly recommended by the Department of Health as a way of recovering from eating disorders. This book is a good starting point and hopefully has pointed you in the right direction.

The next chapter contains some very useful organisations for people suffering from an eating disorder.

Getting better from an eating disorder is not an easy mission – either for the sufferer or for someone trying to help them. Here's wishing you all the best if you are one of the many struggling with a very serious condition. Good luck!

HELPFUL ORGANISATIONS

Eating Disorders Association

103 Prince of Wales Road

Norwich NR1 1DW

Adult help line: 0845 634 1414 (Monday–Friday 8.30am–8.30pm and Saturday 1.00–4.30pm)

Youth line: 0845 634 7650 (Monday–Friday 4.00pm–6.30pm and Saturday 1.00pm–4.30pm)

Email: info@edauk.com

Website: www.edauk.com

This organisation provides information, advice and publications on all aspects of eating disorders including anorexia nervosa, bulimia nervosa, binge eating and related eating disorders. It operates a UK-wide telephone help line for people with an eating disorder, their family, friends and professionals. The youth line offers information, help and support for young people aged 18 years and under.

First Steps to Freedom

7 Avon Court

School Lane

Kenilworth CV8 2GX

Help line: 01926 851 608 (every day 10am–10pm)
Information line: 01926 864 473
Email: info@first-steps.org
Website: www.first-steps.org
This is a confidential help line for people suffering from general anxiety, panic attacks, phobias, obsessive-compulsive disorder, anorexia nervosa and bulimia nervosa, and their carers. It offers counselling, listening, advice, support and information.

Careline
Cardinal Heenan Centre
326 High Road
Ilford
Essex IG1 1QP
Tel: 020 8514 1177 (Monday–Friday 10am–4pm and 7pm–10pm)
Careline provides confidential telephone counselling for children, young people and adults on any issue including eating disorders, depression, loneliness, anxieties and phobias.

Mental Health Foundation
83 Victoria Street
London SW1H 0HW
Tel: 020 7802 0300 (Monday–Friday 10.30am–4.00pm)
Email: mhf@mhf.org.uk
Website: www.mentalhealth.org.uk
The Mental Health Foundation is working to improve the support available for people with mental health problems and people with learning disabilities. It offers information and literature on all aspects of mental health, including where to get help, information about specific mental health problems, treatments and rights.

WEBSITES

Lucy Serpell's Eating Disorders Resources

www.serpell.com/eat.html

This is an informative website with resources on eating disorders including anorexia nervosa, bulimia nervosa, compulsive eating and binge eating, with details of organisations, publications and links to other websites.

The National Centre for Eating Disorders

www.eating-disorders.org.uk

This website contains information available to download, for eating disorders such as binge eating, anorexia nervosa, bulimia nervosa and dieting. It also offers information, counselling and professional training.

Something Fishy Website on Eating Disorders

www.something-fishy.org

Pro-recovery website dedicated to raising awareness about eating disorders, and providing support and information for those with eating disorders and their family and friends.

Weight Concern

www.weightconcern.com

This is a new charity that hopes to address the rising problem of obesity and both the physical and emotional health needs of overweight people. Weight Concern aims to:

- Promote better advice and treatment services for overweight people
- Support research into the treatment and prevention of obesity
- Speak out on behalf of overweight people against prejudice and discrimination.